# HERNANDO DE SOTO

## Peggy Pancella

Heinemann Library
Chicago, Illinois

© 2004 Heinemann Library
a division of Reed Elsevier Inc.
Chicago, Illinois

Customer Service  888-454-2279
Visit our website at www.heinemannlibrary.com

Designed by Lisa Buckley
Maps by John Fleck
Photo research by Alan Gottlieb
Printed and Bound in the United States by Lake Book Manufacturing, Inc.

08 07 06 05 04
10 9 8 7 6 5 4 3 2 1

**Library of Congress Cataloging-in-Publication Data**
Pancella, Peggy
Hernando de Soto / Peggy Pancella.
     p. cm. -- (Historical biographies)
Summary: Presents an overview of Hernando de Soto's life as well as his influence on history and the world.
Includes bibliographical references and index.
  ISBN 1-4034-3702-5 (HC) -- ISBN 1-4034-3710-6 (pbk.)
  1. Soto, Hernando de, ca. 1500-1542--Juvenile literature. 2. America--Discovery and exploration--Spanish--Juvenile literature. 3. Explorers--America--Biography--Juvenile literature. 4. Explorers--Spain--Biography--Juvenile literature. [1. De Soto, Hernando, ca. 1500-1542. 2. America--Discovery and exploration--Spanish. 3. Explorers.]  I. Title. II. Series.
  E125.S7P36 2003
  970.01'6'092--dc21

                              2003005920

**Acknowledgments**
The author and publisher are grateful to the following for permission to reproduce copyright material: Icon, pp. 12, 14, 17, 23, 28 General Research Division/Astor, Lenox and Tilden Foundation/New York Public Library; pp. 4, 15, 18 Hulton Archive/Getty Images; pp. 6, 7 Tom Bean/Corbis; pp. 8, 13 Bettmann/Corbis; pp. 9, 10, 11, 22, 26, 27 North Wind Picture Archives; p. 16 Giraudon/ArtResource, NY; p. 20 Library of Congress/Neg.#LC-USZ62-104322; p. 21 Library of Congress/Neg.#LC-USZ62-104378; p. 24 Library of Congress/Neg.#LC-USZ62-104381; p. 25 Courtesy Arkansas History Commissions; p. 29 Tom Gary/National Park Service.

Cover photograph: Hulton Archive/Getty Images

Special thanks to Michelle Rimsa for her comments in preparation of this book.

Every effort has been made to contact copyright holders of any material reproduced in this book. Any omissions will be rectified in subsequent printings if notice is given to the publisher.

Some words are shown in bold, **like this.** You can find out what they mean by looking in the glossary.

Many names and terms may be found in the pronunciation guide.

For more information on the image of Hernando de Soto that appears on the cover of this book, turn to page 4.

# Contents

# Who Was Hernando de Soto?

Hernando de Soto was a Spanish **explorer** who lived about 500 years ago. He traveled to the Americas in search of riches. He never found the amounts of gold he wanted, but he did visit many places no Europeans had seen before. De Soto's explorations encouraged Spain and other European nations to start **colonies** in the New World.

▲ Hernando de Soto traveled through large areas of North and South America. This drawing of him was made in about 1535.

### The world in de Soto's time

De Soto lived during a time when the world was changing in many ways. People had started to make new kinds of art and music. They had also formed new ideas about science and religion. This period was called the Renaissance, which is a French word that means "rebirth."

At the same time, people were becoming more interested in faraway lands. They wanted to trade for treasures. They also hoped to start colonies or even claim the lands as their own. In 1492, Christopher Columbus proved that it was possible to sail safely across the Atlantic Ocean and back.

After Columbus completed his journeys, many more explorers traveled to the New World. We know these lands today as North America and South America.

### How do we know about Hernando de Soto?

Few records of Hernando de Soto's life survive today. Some of what we know about him comes from his own letters and writings. Some

▲ This map shows Spain, Portugal, and some of the areas where de Soto lived as a young man. It also shows Sanlúcar, the city that de Soto left Spain from in 1538.

information about de Soto comes from stories of his life written by people who knew de Soto well or even traveled with him. Finally, **archaeologists** have visited some of the places that de Soto explored. They have discovered **artifacts** that give clues about his life and work.

| Key dates | |
|---|---|
| about 1500 | Birth of de Soto |
| about 1514 | De Soto goes to Panama with Pedrarias |
| 1531 | De Soto goes to Peru with Pizarro |
| 1539 | De Soto arrives in Florida |
| 1541 | De Soto arrives at the Mississippi River |
| 1542 | Death of de Soto |

# De Soto's Early Life

Hernando de Soto was probably born in about 1500 in Jerez de los Caballeros, Spain. The town is also known simply as Jerez. De Soto's parents both came from old **noble** families, but they were not very rich. De Soto had an older brother, Juan, and two sisters named Catalina and Maria.

### Life in Jerez

Because little information exists on life in small towns during the 1500s, we can only make guesses about de Soto's boyhood. In de Soto's time, Jerez was a village of mostly poor people. The houses were small and built very close together. Much of the town was not very clean, so sicknesses spread quickly. Many people—especially young children—died from illness or starvation.

Although life was hard, people in Jerez managed to enjoy themselves. The town's market was always crowded with people.

▲ This photo shows a town in the Extremadura region, where de Soto grew up.

Musicians and other entertainers performed in the streets. The church was also important in town life. Most of the people were **Roman Catholic.**

## Preparing for adult life

Most people like de Soto learned to read and write. De Soto probably also studied subjects such as math and history. This knowledge would help him get a job when he grew up. His older brother would receive the family's land and money. Hernando would have to go to work. His parents wanted him to be a priest or a lawyer.

▲ This photo shows part of the mountainous area near where de Soto lived as a boy.

But Hernando was more interested in riding horses and having adventures. He decided to become a *hidalgo*—a sort of **knight.** These proud and honorable men fought to defend their land. They also tried to win riches, often by robbing or fighting their enemies. De Soto was ready to fight to find his fortune.

### The Extremadura region

Hernando de Soto's hometown was in a mountainous part of western Spain called Extremadura, meaning "very hard" in Spanish. The land is very dry and rocky, so not much can grow or live there. The people of Extremadura had to be smart and tough to survive. Many people who grew up there chose to leave as soon as they were able.

# The Age of Exploration

De Soto lived at a time when people were eager to visit new places. He probably heard stories about **explorers** when he was growing up. These tales made de Soto interested in having adventures of his own.

▲ This painting shows Christopher Columbus leaving Spain.

### Earlier explorations

One explorer de Soto probably admired was Christopher Columbus. Columbus was an Italian who made four **voyages** for Spain, beginning in 1492. He had hoped to find a way to sail to lands known as the Indies so the Spanish could trade goods there. Instead, he discovered parts of the Americas.

Juan Ponce de León and Vasco Núñez de Balboa made major discoveries while de Soto was growing up. Balboa crossed the country of Panama. He became the first person to reach the Pacific Ocean. Balboa was also probably from Jerez, so he became a hero to de Soto.

## Getting started

Many explorers of de Soto's time claimed they made their journeys for "God, gold, and glory." They wanted to teach native peoples about the **Christian** religion, to find many treasures, and to become famous. King Ferdinand and Queen Isabella of Spain supported these ideas. They offered explorers money and supplies for travel. In return, the explorers claimed the new lands for Spain. The king and queen also wanted to share in any treasures the explorers might find.

In about 1514, de Soto moved to Seville, a great city in Spain. There, he was hired to work for a man named Pedro Arias de Avila, who was usually called Pedrarias. Soon after, Pedrarias was made **governor** of Darién, Panama, a new Spanish settlement in Central America. Pedrarias took de Soto along as a **page**.

▼ Juan Ponce de Léon, seen below, discovered a new land, which he named La Florida, in 1513.

### Pedrarias

Pedrarias was known for being very cruel to others. People obeyed him because they were afraid of him. Earlier, Pedrarias had helped the Spanish win an important battle. But he was almost 70 years old when he was sent to Darién. He did not know how to rule well, and most people disliked him because he was so mean.

# Early Adventures

De Soto had lived his whole life in the same small town. Now he was going far away. He would miss his family and friends, but he was ready to have new adventures.

### Life in Panama

It took almost two months to get to Panama. Once there, de Soto began serving Pedrarias as a **page.** One of his jobs was guarding Pedrarias's wife and two young daughters. De Soto grew close to the family, and they considered him a trusted friend.

De Soto also helped to battle the native peoples. Pedrarias and many others kept fighting to get gold and treasures. In de Soto's first battle, he fought so well that he was given his own horse. His bold style and great bravery soon made him successful. Pedrarias rewarded de Soto with gold and his own **slaves.**

▲ Pedrarias attacked many of the native people in Panama.

### De Soto and Balboa

One of the people de Soto was eager to see in Panama was his countryman, Vasco Núñez de Balboa. Balboa had been in Panama for some time before de Soto arrived. Pedrarias was cruel to the natives. Balboa was less cruel.

Two or three years after his arrival, de Soto finally got to meet Balboa. Balboa liked the young de Soto and trained him in sword fighting. But the lessons did not last for long. Pedrarias envied Balboa. He did not want Balboa to take over. So Pedrarias had Balboa's head cut off. De Soto was sad and angry about Balboa's death. However, he could not say anything bad to Pedrarias. De Soto was afraid that Pedrarias might hurt him, too.

▶ Vasco Núñez de Balboa is shown here seeing the Pacific Ocean for the first time and claiming it for Spain.

### Amadis of Gaul

A book called The **Virtuous Knight** Amadis of Gaul was very popular in Europe during de Soto's lifetime. It told about a young boy who became a knight. He fell in love with a king's daughter but could not marry her until he had passed many challenges. De Soto's life was like Amadis's in some ways.

# A Rising Star

Even though he did not like the way Pedrarias treated others, de Soto continued to serve his master faithfully. Pedrarias admired de Soto's bravery. He knew he could count on de Soto when help was needed.

## Adventure in Nicaragua

In 1523, there were problems in Nicaragua, a country near Panama. Pedrarias decided to take over Nicaragua and rule the country himself. He chose Francisco Fernández de Córdoba to lead his soldiers into Nicaragua. De Soto was second in command of the soldiers.

Once the soldiers reached Nicaragua, more trouble began. Córdoba decided to take over the land for himself instead of letting Pedrarias rule. De Soto thought this was wrong. But Córdoba put de Soto in jail

▲ Francisco Fernández de Córdoba is seen here accepting a gift from a group of Indians.

before he could do anything about it. Then a friend helped de Soto and others escape. They sneaked back to Panama to tell Pedrarias what had happened. Pedrarias was so angry that he went to Nicaragua and had Córdoba killed.

## A comfortable life

Pedrarias chose to stay in Nicaragua for a while. De Soto and some friends came back to Nicaragua as well. Over the next few years, de Soto and his closest friends tried to get rich. They made some journeys for Pedrarias, looking for gold and treasures. They also got involved in the businesses of **shipping** and gold **mining**. The men earned a lot of money in these businesses. They became important, respected people.

But de Soto wanted more adventures. A man he knew, Francisco Pizarro, wanted to go to Peru to conquer a group of people who he believed had great riches. De Soto dreamed of going along. However, Pedrarias stopped him. De Soto was unhappy, but again he felt he could not disobey Pedrarias.

▲ This artwork shows Spanish explorer Hernán Cortés.

### Cortés and the Aztecs

During the years de Soto was with Pedrarias, many Spanish explorers tried to find riches in the New World. Most of them were inspired by the story of Hernán Cortés. In 1519, Cortés had led his men into Mexico. There, they defeated the Aztec people. The treasures they found made Cortés very rich. In all of Spain, only the king had more money than Cortés did!

# Conquest in Peru

In 1531, something happened that finally allowed de Soto to follow his dream. Pedrarias died. Pedrarias was about 90 years old. Now, de Soto was free to make his own decisions—and he chose to go to Peru with Pizarro.

### Meeting the Incas

It took the Spanish troops a long time to reach Peru, where the Incas lived. They finally arrived in the fall of 1532. It was a good time to attack because the Incas were having problems. Their old ruler and many other people had died from a disease. The ruler's two sons fought each other until one of them, Atahualpa, killed the other and took power. All this trouble meant that the Incas were not ready to fight any battles.

▲ De Soto is shown here leading a charge into a battle against the Incas in Peru.

De Soto led a group of men to meet Atahualpa at the Inca city of Cajamarca. De Soto knew that the Incas had probably never seen a horse, so he thought they would be afraid of them. He tried to scare Atahualpa by riding very close to him, but the Inca leader did not move.

## Riches at last

Atahualpa did not expect an attack. The Spanish soldiers killed thousands of his men. The soldiers let Atahualpa live for months while they collected the Incas' gold and silver. One night while de Soto was away from camp, the Spanish soldiers killed Atahualpa.

Next, the Spanish soldiers took over Cuzco, a city several hundred miles to the southeast. De Soto got a large amount of gold and silver. Pizarro made de Soto the **lieutenant governor** of Cuzco. De Soto was finally rich and successful.

▼ Atahualpa promised gold and silver to the Spanish soldiers if they spared his life.

### The Incas

The Incas had lived peacefully in Peru for many years. Their **empire** stretched for 2,000 miles (3,200 kilometers) along the Andes Mountains, from northern Ecuador to central Chile. The Incas used stone to pave roads and build strong bridges. They also built beautiful houses and **temples.** They used gold and silver to make masks, jewelry, and other items.

# A Hero's Welcome

De Soto stayed in Cuzco for four years. He had a fine home and many riches. But not many exciting things happened in the city, and de Soto was bored. He decided it was time to return home.

## Back to Spain

De Soto finally returned to Spain in 1536, after more than twenty years in the New World. The people in Spain welcomed him as a hero because of his bravery and the riches he had won.

De Soto moved into a large house in Seville and hired many servants to help him. He gave some of his money to friends as gifts. He was so rich that he even lent money to the king! De Soto also married Isabel de Bobadilla, the daughter of Pedrarias.

## Longing for action

For a short time, de Soto enjoyed a peaceful life with his new wife. After only a few months, though, his love for adventure won out.

◄ **This painting shows the Spanish city of Seville.**

◀ **De Soto married this woman, Isabel de Bobadilla, in 1536.**

De Soto was only 36 years old. He thought he was too young to retire. He also still wanted to lead his own men instead of working for others.

De Soto asked Charles I, who was Spain's king, for permission to explore lands in South America. However, Charles already had several strong Spanish leaders there. Instead, Charles asked de Soto to explore a large new land north of Cuba— La Florida, discovered earlier by Juan Ponce de León. De Soto could build a **colony** there and search the land for riches. He would become *adelantado,* or **governor**, of both Cuba and La Florida. In return, Charles would reward him with land and money.

### Álvar Núñez Cabeza de Vaca

In Seville, de Soto visited several old friends who got him interested in traveling again. One man, Álvar Núñez Cabeza de Vaca, had been to La Florida in about 1527. Most of the 300 men on his trip had died from illness, starvation, or accidents. Only four men survived. Cabeza de Vaca wandered the land for years.

# Governor of Florida

Word spread quickly about de Soto's trip. Many men were interested because they hoped to find great riches in the New World. De Soto, Isabel, and about 700 men left the Spanish port of Sanlúcar on April 7, 1538. It took more than a month to cross the Atlantic Ocean. In Havana, Cuba, de Soto's men restocked their supplies. They also bought some hunting dogs, some hogs to eat for food, and 230 horses.

▼ **De Soto's men are shown in this drawing setting up camp on the coast of Florida in 1539.**

### *Arriving in Florida*

De Soto's men explored the coast of Florida and looked for a good place to land their large ships. In May of 1539, de Soto set out, leaving Isabel to rule Cuba in his place. He claimed the new land for Spain.

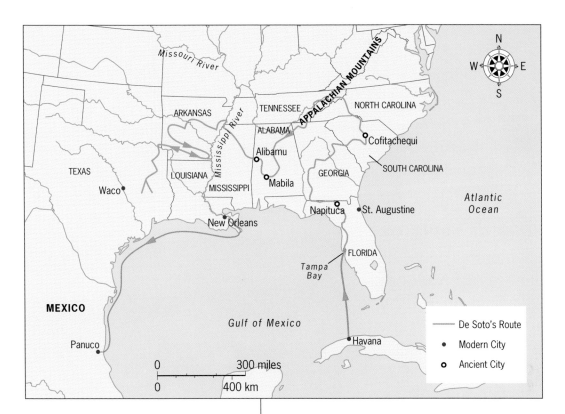

▲ **The state borders did not exist at the time, but this map shows where de Soto and his men traveled in America.**

De Soto's men explored the nearby land and soon met a small group of Indians. The soldiers tried to attack, but one of the men called out to them in Spanish. It was Juan Ortiz, a survivor from an earlier group of **explorers**. He had been living with some friendly Indians. Now Juan joined de Soto as a guide and an **interpreter**.

### Facing difficulties

However, other Indians living nearby did not trust de Soto and his men. They hid in the **swamps** and shot arrows at the Spanish scouts. It was hard for the Spanish to fight back. They were hot, tired, and hungry, and they did not know the land very well.

The Indians' fighting kept de Soto's men from getting much done. Some of the men were so unhappy that they quit working for de Soto. Others went back to Cuba for more supplies. Worst of all, no one had found any gold or treasures yet. But de Soto would not give up.

# Searching for Riches

The Spanish troops kept traveling, trying to find treasures. They stole food from the Indians or found what they could. The soldiers were determined to succeed.

## Attack at Napituca

In September 1539, de Soto reached Napituca, a village in the northern part of Florida. His men were tired and hungry, but they heard that a Timucuan Indian *cacique,* or chief, was preparing a feast for them. However, Juan Ortiz understood the Timucuan language. He realized that the feast was really a trick—the Indians planned to attack. When the soldiers met the Timucuans on an open field, de Soto gave a signal, and the Spanish attacked. They captured many of the Timucuans, including the *cacique,* Vitachuco.

▲ Vitachuco pretended to be friendly so the Spanish soldiers would trust him. But he really wanted to attack them when they came near.

De Soto wanted some Indians to come along as his servants. He tried to show that he was kind by treating the Indians well. But after the meal, the *cacique* suddenly attacked. Spanish guards rescued de Soto and killed Vitachuco. The Spanish and Timucuans fought most of the night until the Spanish finally won.

## La Señora

Afterward, de Soto and his men set up a winter camp. They asked the Indians where to find riches. One man told them about a place called Cofitachequi, a settlement near the present-day city of Camden, South Carolina. A powerful woman named La Señora ruled there. In March 1540, the men began the difficult trip to her village.

La Señora welcomed the soldiers. She offered food and traded gifts with de Soto. However, La Señora had no gold, only pearls to share. The men took two handfuls each and loaded a small chest for King Charles. Despite La Señora's kindness, the men kidnapped her as they left the town. But she and her servants later escaped. They also took the chest of pearls with them!

▲ The Indian La Señora gave de Soto a pearl necklace when he arrived.

## Problems in Florida

The Spanish were lucky to succeed at all in Florida. They did not know the land, and were not used to the Indians' way of fighting by surprise attack. The Indians could also shoot arrows faster than Spanish soldiers could fire their guns. The soldiers had to wear hot, uncomfortable **armor** all the time in case of attack. They were usually too busy or tired to prepare the little food they had. They often ate corn because it was easy to find and did not need to be cooked.

# More Conflicts

Without any natives to guide them, de Soto and his men wandered around on their own. Some Indians greeted them kindly and offered food and servants. Other times, though, they were not so friendly.

### Dealings with the natives

De Soto made problems with the Indians by treating them harshly. King Charles had asked him to be peaceful with the natives.

However, de Soto and his men stole food, kidnapped *caciques,* and forced Indians to travel with them as **slaves.** If the Indians tried to fight back, the Spanish soldiers attacked fiercely. They killed many natives and destroyed their villages.

### Battle with Tascaluza

The Spanish soldiers headed south toward the Gulf of Mexico. Along the way, they captured Tascaluza, who was a powerful Indian chief. Tascaluza promised to provide help. He secretly sent messengers to his village, called Mabila. He told his people to prepare a surprise attack.

▲ De Soto and his men are seen here taking a break from their travels.

22

When de Soto neared Mabila, some of his men warned him to be

▲ De Soto and his men were lucky to survive the fighting at Mabila. They lost 80 horses and much of their food and belongings.

careful. They had seen the Indians gathering supplies and strengthening the town's wall. But de Soto did not think it was a trap. He led his horsemen toward the town.

Thousands of Indians attacked with arrows and spears. The surprised soldiers ran away quickly. However, their native servants ran inside the village, taking the soldiers' food and supplies with them. De Soto angrily ordered his men to charge. After more than nine hours of fighting, about 2,500 Indians were dead. The Spanish lost only 22 men, with about 150 others—including de Soto—**wounded.**

### Ships to the rescue

Some of the Indians de Soto captured gave him good news. They had seen Spanish ships near the coast only about 80 miles (130 kilometers) away. De Soto knew these ships were probably bringing men and supplies from Cuba. He needed these things badly. However, de Soto decided not to tell anyone about the ships. He worried that his men would try to return to Cuba. Then he would not be able to talk them into **exploring** any more.

# The Great River

De Soto led his tired troops northwest to a town near the present-day city of Mobile, Alabama. There, they made camp for the winter. They also met members of a local group of Indians called the Chickasaws.

### Trouble with the Chickasaws

When de Soto prepared to start traveling again, he asked the Chickasaw chief to send 200 men along as servants. The chief agreed, but de Soto felt nervous. He posted lookouts and warned his men to be ready for a fight.

▲ The first battle with the Chickasaws was one of the most difficult battles that de Soto's men fought.

Soon after, the Chickasaws quietly surrounded the camp very early one morning. Then they attacked, firing flaming arrows and shouting. The surprised Spanish troops were not ready for battle and ran in all directions. De Soto had worn his **armor** to bed. He and a few other soldiers were able to fight off the Indians. But the camp was burned to the ground, and their weapons were damaged.

The survivors set up a new camp not far away. They tried to fix their weapons. Cold, wet, and hungry, the men watched for another attack. When the Chickasaws tried again more than a week later, the Spanish soldiers were ready. They fought hard and defeated the Indians.

## Finding the Mississippi

De Soto and his men kept traveling. Many men were sick or hurt, so they had to go slowly. Finally, on about May 9, 1541, the soldiers reached the bank of the Mississippi River near what is now the state of Tennessee. No Europeans were known to have been there before. De Soto was amazed at how big the river was.

The men set up camp and built four large **barges** to float across the river. They spent much of the summer and fall exploring near the river's western bank in what is now the state of Arkansas. When winter came, they built a camp nearby and settled in.

▲ This artwork shows what it might have looked like when de Soto saw the Mississippi for the first time.

### The Mississippi River

The Mississippi is the largest river in the United States. Only the Nile, in Africa, and the Amazon, in South America, are longer. The Mississippi flows about 2,340 miles (3,770 kilometers) from its **source** in Minnesota to its **mouth** near New Orleans, Louisiana. There, it empties into the Gulf of Mexico. The Mississippi is part of a huge system of rivers that stretches across much of the United States. Today, many things are shipped along the river.

# The Adventurer Dies

The winter of 1541 was long and hard. Many men died, including Juan Ortiz. Without him, it would be harder for de Soto to communicate with the natives.

### End of a journey

De Soto's men were tired and discouraged. They had not found riches, and their supplies were running low. Also, more than half of the men were gone. Some had been killed by Indians or died of illness, and some had run away. The soldiers did not want to **explore** any more.

In March 1542, the group headed back toward the Mississippi River. De Soto became very sick, probably with **malaria.** He thanked the men for their bravery and chose a new leader for them. De Soto died on May 21, 1542.

The soldiers were afraid the Indians might attack if they knew de Soto was dead. So, the soldiers buried him at night. The next night, they decided it would be safer to sink de Soto in the Mississippi River. So, they dug up the body and sank it in the river.

▲ De Soto's men made sure the Indians could not find his body by sinking him in the Mississippi River.

## Changes of plans

De Soto's men planned to head toward Mexico. They went by land instead of water, still hoping they might find some riches on the way.

▲ This drawing shows de Soto's men sailing down the Mississippi River after de Soto's death.

After five months, the men were near what is now Waco, Texas. However, they had found no treasures. They headed back almost 400 miles (650 kilometers) to the Mississippi. The men built boats and sailed down the river, often stopping to raid Indian villages. The Indians attacked the boats throughout the trip. When the men reached the Gulf of Mexico, they followed the coastline to a Mexican town called Pánuco. The 311 survivors were tired and starving, but they were safe.

### Tricking the Indians

De Soto had tried to show his power by telling the local Indians that he was **immortal**. Some of the Indians looked up to him as a god. When de Soto died, his men pretended he was still alive. They lied by saying that their leader was visiting his father, the Sun, and would be back soon. The soldiers also marched around and kept busy so it looked like de Soto was there giving them orders.

# After de Soto

In Pánuco, de Soto's men received food, medicine, and new clothes. Many of the men sailed home to Europe, but nearly half stayed in the New World—some in Mexico and some in Peru. In Cuba, de Soto's wife, Isabel, heard of his death. She was heartbroken and alone, and she died not long after.

### De Soto the failure

Most people of the time saw de Soto as a big failure. He did not find gold or treasures in Florida, and he did not become famous. His rough treatment made the natives his enemies, and they caused trouble for future **explorers** as well. De Soto also did not start a **colony** as King Charles had asked, and he lost half of his men along the way. Even those men who survived did not all agree that de Soto had been a good leader.

### De Soto's gifts to the future

However, de Soto actually did many important things. He was first to explore large parts of what is now the southeastern United States. He and his men visited parts of ten future states. De Soto also is believed to be one of the first Europeans to see the mighty Mississippi River.

▶ Hernando de Soto failed to see some of his dreams come true, but he also accomplished things no one had before.

THE NATIONAL SOCIETY OF THE COLONIAL DAMES OF AMERICA IN FLORIDA

NEAR HERE HERNANDO DESOTO WITH HIS MEN LANDED MAY 30,1539 AND BEGAN HIS MARCH WESTWARD TO THE MISSISSIPPI RIVER. THIS MARKER COMMEMORATES THE 400TH ANNIVERSARY OF HIS ARRIVAL ON THE SHORES OF FLORIDA.

▲ This trail marker shows the beginning of the path that de Soto and his men probably took through America.

After de Soto and other explorers failed to find gold in the New World, Spain decided to quit looking. The Spanish concentrated on Mexico instead. They already had some settlements there. They developed farms, ranches, and **mining** businesses that made a lot of money.

Several of de Soto's men who wrote about their travels included details about the land, people, plants, and animals they found. This information provides a record of what the area was like before many settlers arrived. It also encouraged more people to go to those places.

Today, there is a national park near Tampa Bay that honors de Soto and his exploration. Several cities also share his name. Now, this brave soldier and explorer is remembered for his successes after all.

# Glossary

**adelantado** Spanish governor in the New World

**archaeologist** person who finds out about the past by studying the remains of buildings and other objects

**armor** special clothing or covering worn to protect the body

**artifact** object that was made or used by humans in the past

**barge** flat-bottomed boat

**cacique** chief of an Indian group in Mexico, the Caribbean, and parts of the southeastern United States

**Christian** person who believes in the teachings of Jesus Christ

**colony** settlement founded by a country in another place

**empire** large land or group of lands ruled by one person or government

**explorer** person who travels to new places

**governor** person who rules a city or land for another person, such as a king

**hidalgo** low-ranking Spanish noble soldier

**immortal** never going to have to die

**interpreter** person who translates from one language to another

**knight** soldier who serves a king or other master

**lieutenant governor** person who is second in command over an area

**malaria** illness causing fever and chills, usually spread by mosquitoes

**mining** digging in the ground to collect gold, coal, or other substances

**mouth** place where a river flows into another body of water

**noble** person of high birth or rank

**page** young person training to be a knight

**Roman Catholic** Christian person who is under the authority of the pope

**shipping** transporting items from place to place

**slave** servant who is the property of his or her master or mistress

**source** place where a river starts to flow

**swamp** soft, wet ground

**temple** building in which people worship a god or gods

**virtuous** doing what is right and not sinful

**voyage** journey from one place to another

**wounded** hurt

# Time Line

| | |
|---|---|
| 1492 | Christopher Columbus makes his first **voyage** to the New World |
| about 1500 | Hernando de Soto is born |
| about 1514 | De Soto goes to Panama with Pedrarias |
| 1532 | De Soto and Francisco Pizarro attack the Incas in Peru |
| 1533 | De Soto becomes **lieutenant governor** of Cuzco |
| 1536 | De Soto returns to Spain and marries Isabel de Bobadilla |
| 1538 | De Soto leads his ships to Cuba |
| 1539 | De Soto's men reach Florida |
| 1541 | De Soto reaches the Mississippi River |
| 1542 | De Soto dies |

# Pronunciation Guide

| Word | You say |
|---|---|
| *adelantado* | AH-deh-lahn-TAH-do |
| Atahualpa | AH-tah-HWAHL-pah |
| Vasco Núñez de Balboa | VAHS-ko  NOON-yez  deh  bal-BO-uh |
| Isabel de Bobadilla | EES-ah-bell  deh  bo-bah-DEE-yah |
| *cacique* | kuh-SEEK |
| Cajamarca | KAH-hah-MAR-kuh |
| Cofitachequi | ko-FEET-ah-cheh-KEE |
| Cuzco | KOOS-ko |
| Extremadura | es-TREH-mah-DOO-rah |
| *hidalgo* | ee-DAHL-go |
| Jerez de los Caballeros | hair-ESS  deh  LOHS  kah-bah-YAIR-ose |
| Juan Ortiz | HWAN  or-TEESE |
| Pedrarias | peh-DRAIR-ee-ahs |
| Juan Ponce de León | HWAN  PAHNSE  deh  lay-OWN |
| Timucuan | tee-MOO-koo-AHN |
| Vitachuco | vee-tah-CHOO-ko |

# More Books to Read

Heinrichs, Ann. *De Soto: Hernando de Soto Explores the Southeast.* Minneapolis, Minn.: Compass Point Books, 2002.

Heinrichs, Ann. *Ponce de Leon: Juan Ponce de Leon Searches for the Fountain of Youth.* Minneapolis, Minn.: Compass Point Books, 2002.

Pancella, Peggy. *Christopher Columbus.* Chicago: Heinemann Library, 2003.

# Index